JR. GRAPHIC ANCIENT CIVILIZATIONS

EVERYDAY LIFE IN
ANCIENT EGYPT

KIRSTEN HOLM

PowerKiDS
press

New York

Published in 2012 by The Rosen Publishing Group, Inc.

29 East 21st Street, New York, NY 10010

First Edition

Editor: Joanne Randolph

Book Design: Planman Technologies

Illustrations: Planman Technologies

Library of Congress Cataloging-in-Publication Data

Holm, Kirsten C. (Kirsten Campbell)

Everyday life in ancient Egypt / by Kirsten Campbell Holm. — 1st ed.

p. cm. — (Jr. graphic ancient civilizations)

Includes index.

ISBN 978-1-4488-6216-0 (library binding) — ISBN 978-1-4488-6391-4 (pbk.) — ISBN 978-1-4488-6392-1 (6-pack)

1. Egypt—Civilization—To 332 B.C.—Juvenile literature. 2. Egypt—Social life and customs—To 332 B.C.—Juvenile literature. 3. Egypt—Antiquities—Juvenile literature. I. Title. II. Series: Jr. graphic ancient civilizations.

DT61.H56 2012

932'.01—dc23

2011027624

Manufactured in the United States of America

CPSIA Compliance Information: Batch #PLW2102PK: For Further Information contact Rosen Publishing, New York, New York at 1-800-237-9932.

Contents

Historical Background   3

Everyday Life in Ancient Egypt   4

Did You Know?   22

Glossary   23

Index and Web Sites   24

Historical Background

Ancient Egypt was the narrow strip of land that lay on each side of the Nile. Every year, the Nile overflowed its banks. When the waters withdrew, they left behind a rich layer of **silt**. Egyptians called their country the Black Land because of this regular deposit of fertile soil. Life in ancient Egypt was built on the yearly cycle of flood, called inundation, followed by planting and harvesting.

Pepi II was Egypt's longest-ruling king. He became king at the age of six, and scholars differ as to whether he reigned for 64 or for 94 years. Although we cannot be sure of the dates, he probably lived from around 2275 to 2175 BC. He was the last important king of the period of Egyptian history called the Old Kingdom. During the reign of Pepi II, Egypt experienced a long **drought**. The drought resulted in poor crops and an **economic decline** for Egypt. After his death, there was a period of **chaos** and war. His **funerary complex** is located in Sakkara South.

EVERYDAY LIFE IN
ANCIENT EGYPT

2200 BC, DURING THE REIGN OF PEPI II. A WORKER'S VILLAGE NEAR SAKKARA, EGYPT.

ANCIENT EGYPT WAS THE FERTILE LAND ALONG THE NILE, LAND KNOWN FOR ITS KINGS AND PYRAMIDS.

IMHOTEP, A BOY FROM ANCIENT EGYPT, ROSE FROM HIS SLEEPING MAT. HE AND HIS FAMILY HAD SLEPT ON THE ROOF OF THEIR HOUSE BECAUSE IT WAS COOLER THERE THAN INSIDE.

IMHOTEP'S FATHER WAS AN ARCHITECT WORKING ON THE GROUP OF PYRAMIDS AND TEMPLES WHERE PEPI II, EGYPT'S KING, WOULD BE BURIED. IMHOTEP'S FAMILY LIVED IN THE WORKMEN'S VILLAGE NEARBY.

THE WATERS OF THE NILE ARE RISING. WHEN THE LAND IS FLOODED, I WILL GO TO SCHOOL AT THE TEMPLE.

YOU WILL TRAIN TO BE AN ARCHITECT, JUST AS I DID.

MALE AND FEMALE EGYPTIANS WORE MAKEUP AND BEAUTIFUL JEWELRY. THEY ALSO WORE **AMULETS** TO PROTECT THEM FROM EVIL.

LET ME SHOW YOU HOW TO PAINT YOUR EYES WITH KOHL. THE PAINT WILL MAKE YOUR EYES LOOK BIGGER.

LIKE OTHER WEALTHY EGYPTIAN FAMILIES, IMHOTEP'S FAMILY BEGAN THE DAY WITH A BREAKFAST OF DATES, FIGS, BREAD, AND CHEESE.

ON MY WAY TO WORK THIS MORNING, I WILL TAKE AN OFFERING TO THE **SHRINE** OF MY PARENTS.

I WILL HAVE THE SERVANTS PREPARE FOOD FOR YOU.

MANY EGYPTIANS HAD SERVANTS, AND WEALTHY EGYPTIANS HAD A STAFF TO HELP IN THE HOUSE. BESIDES COOKING AND CLEANING, SERVANTS KEPT LIZARDS, SNAKES, RATS, AND MICE OUT OF THE HOUSE.

THERE ARE SO MANY THINGS TO BE DONE EVERY DAY, EVEN WITH SERVANTS TO HELP.

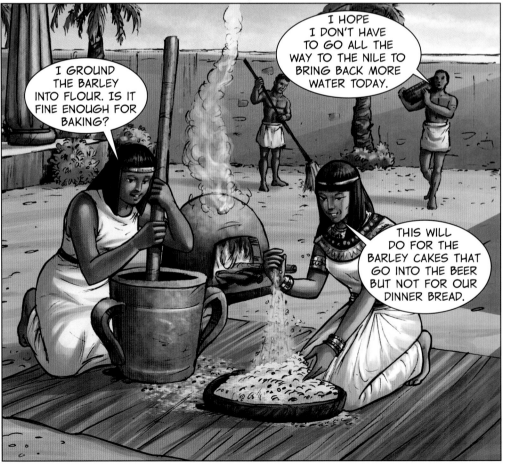

I GROUND THE BARLEY INTO FLOUR. IS IT FINE ENOUGH FOR BAKING?

I HOPE I DON'T HAVE TO GO ALL THE WAY TO THE NILE TO BRING BACK MORE WATER TODAY.

THIS WILL DO FOR THE BARLEY CAKES THAT GO INTO THE BEER BUT NOT FOR OUR DINNER BREAD.

FLAX WAS SPUN INTO THREAD SO THAT IT COULD BE WOVEN.

THIS IS HARD WORK, BUT WE HAVE TO MAKE A LOT OF THREAD FOR THE LOOM.

THE FLAX THREADS WERE THEN WOVEN INTO LINEN CLOTH.

MY LINEN CLOTH SELLS WELL IN THE MARKETS OF MEMPHIS.

SOMEDAY MY CLOTH WILL BE JUST AS BEAUTIFUL. PERHAPS I WILL BECOME A SEAMSTRESS.

EGYPTIAN WOMEN COULD WORK AS PRIESTESSES, ESPECIALLY FOR NEITH, THE GODDESS OF WEAVING. PRIESTESSES WORKED AT THE TEMPLE DEVOTED TO THEIR GOD OR GODDESS FOR SEVERAL MONTHS A YEAR.

I AM HONORED TO BE A PRIESTESS FOR NEITH. IN THE MONTHS THAT I AM NOT WORKING AT THE TEMPLE, I CAN TEACH WEAVING AND MAKE MORE LINEN TO SELL.

I LIKE BEING YOUR **APPRENTICE** HERE AT HOME. ONE DAY I WANT TO WORK AT THE TEMPLE, TOO.

I WILL SELL MANY LOAVES OF BREAD THIS SEASON.

I AM SELLING CLOTH IN MEMPHIS NEXT MARKET DAY. I WILL GET TO BE OUTSIDE ALL DAY, JUST LIKE THE MEN.

IMHOTEP WENT WITH HIS FATHER TO THE PYRAMID SITE EACH DAY. ARCHITECTS WERE ALSO **SCRIBES**, SO IMHOTEP HELPED HIS FATHER CARRY TOOLS FOR BOTH JOBS.

THE WOMEN WEAVE, WHILE WE WORK OUTSIDE IN THE HEAT. SOMETIMES I MISS MY SCHOOL DAYS. WE SPENT THE DAY INSIDE LEARNING TO WRITE.

I ALREADY KNOW SOME SYMBOLS. I WANT TO BE A SCRIBE TO THE KING OR AN ARCHITECT, LIKE YOU.

A SCRIBE'S TOOLS INCLUDED INK, BRUSHES, AND TOOLS TO REPAIR THE BRUSHES. AN ARCHITECT'S TOOLS INCLUDED A PLUMB LINE, A SQUARE, AND A MEASURING STICK.

ON OUR WAY TO THE CONSTRUCTION SITE, WE MUST HONOR MY PARENTS. I USED TO GO WITH MY OWN FATHER TO MAKE OFFERINGS.

NOW I CAN GO WITH YOU.

EGYPTIANS BELIEVED IN LIFE AFTER DEATH. OFFERINGS TO ANCESTORS INCLUDED GRAPES AND WINE FOR THE *KA*, THE SPIRIT THAT MADE IT POSSIBLE FOR THE PERSON TO ENJOY LIFE AFTER DEATH.

THAT PYRAMID WAS BUILT BY THE GREAT IMHOTEP. YOU WERE NAMED FOR HIM.

MAYBE I WILL BE A GREAT ARCHITECT, TOO, AND BUILD PYRAMIDS FOR OUR NEXT KING.

IT TOOK MANY YEARS AND HUNDREDS OF WORKERS TO BUILD A PYRAMID COMPLEX.

THE PYRAMIDS AND TEMPLES FOR PEPI II HAD BEEN UNDER CONSTRUCTION FOR MANY YEARS, EVEN BEFORE IMHOTEP'S FATHER BECAME AN ARCHITECT. **RITUALS** WERE OFTEN PERFORMED THROUGHOUT THE CONSTRUCTION.

THIS PYRAMID FOR PEPI II LINKS OUR WORLD HERE TO THE AFTERLIFE THE KING WILL ENJOY.

WITH ONLY A FEW SIMPLE TOOLS, EGYPTIAN ARCHITECTS DESIGNED LASTING MONUMENTS. THE PLUMB LINE WAS USED TO MAKE STRAIGHT, VERTICAL LINES. THE SQUARE WAS USED TO MAKE SURE THAT CORNERS WERE PERFECTLY FORMED.

SOON THERE WILL BE MANY WORKMEN HERE.

THIS DOOR IS SQUARE. WHAT A GREAT JOB YOU HAVE DONE, FATHER.

IT TAKES MANY LABORERS TO BUILD A PYRAMID.

WHILE THEIR FARMLAND IS FLOODED, FARMERS SERVE THE KING AND COME HERE TO WORK. WHILE THEY ARE WORKING HERE, THE KING FEEDS AND CARES FOR THEM.

THE NILE WAS USED AS A HIGHWAY. BARGES BROUGHT CUT STONES FROM THE QUARRIES IN THE SOUTH TO BUILD THE PYRAMIDS.

PRIESTS OBSERVED THE STARS TO DETERMINE WHICH WAY WAS NORTH. THE LINES OF THE PYRAMID'S BASE RUN STRAIGHT NORTH, SOUTH, EAST, AND WEST.

WORKMEN FLOODED CHANNELS WITH WATER. THE GROUND WAS EVENED OFF TO THE WATERLINE SO THAT THE PYRAMID COULD BE BUILT ON LEVEL GROUND.

WHEN THE WALLS WERE SMOOTH, ARTISTS AND SCRIBES WENT TO WORK, COVERING THE SPACE WITH PICTURES AND WRITTEN PRAYERS.

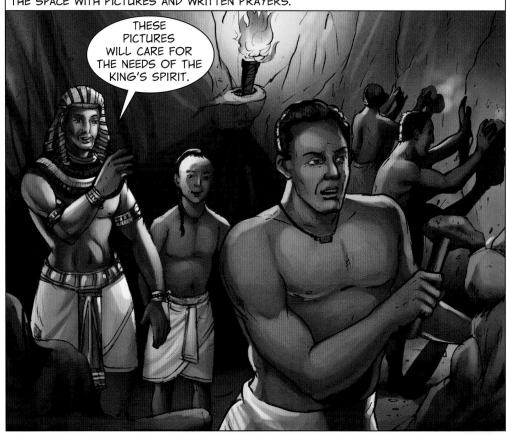

THE WRITING AND PICTURES PROVIDED ALL THE NECESSARY SPELLS AND PRAYERS FOR THE DEAD.

CARVINGS AND PICTURES IN THE PYRAMID SHOWED THE KING'S ACTIVITIES.

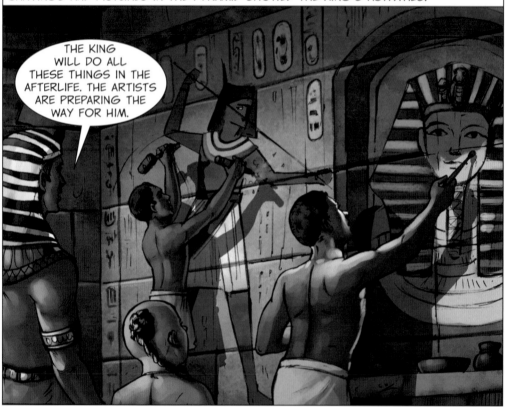

THE KING WILL DO ALL THESE THINGS IN THE AFTERLIFE. THE ARTISTS ARE PREPARING THE WAY FOR HIM.

EGYPTIANS BELIEVED THAT WHEN THE KING DIED, HIS HEART WOULD BE WEIGHED BY ANUBIS, THE GOD OF THE UNDERWORLD. HEARTS THAT WERE OUT OF BALANCE WERE EATEN BY A MONSTER.

THE KING'S HEART PERFECTLY BALANCES THE FEATHER OF TRUTH.

NO MONSTER WILL EAT OUR KING'S HEART!

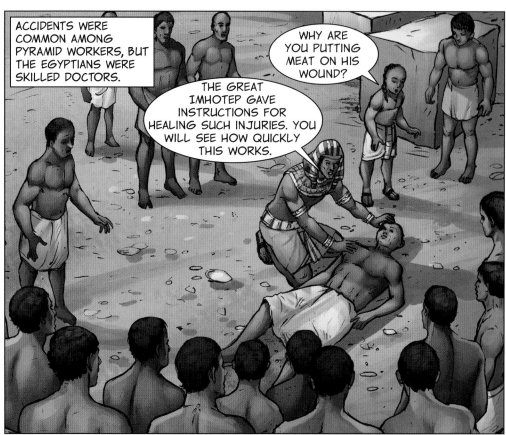

ACCIDENTS WERE COMMON AMONG PYRAMID WORKERS, BUT THE EGYPTIANS WERE SKILLED DOCTORS.

WHY ARE YOU PUTTING MEAT ON HIS WOUND?

THE GREAT IMHOTEP GAVE INSTRUCTIONS FOR HEALING SUCH INJURIES. YOU WILL SEE HOW QUICKLY THIS WORKS.

THE SHAPE OF THE PYRAMIDS WAS A SYMBOL OF EGYPTIAN SOCIETY. THE KING WAS AT THE TOP. BELOW HIM WERE THE NOBLES, THE FARMERS, AND THEN THE LABORERS.

THE JOB OF THE KING IS TO MAINTAIN BALANCE AND ORDER.

OUR LIFE WILL GO ON SMOOTHLY, AS IT ALWAYS HAS.

WHEN THE KING DIED, HIS BODY UNDERWENT THE RITUAL OF MUMMIFICATION. THIS PRESERVED THE BODY FOR THE KING'S USE IN THE AFTERLIFE.

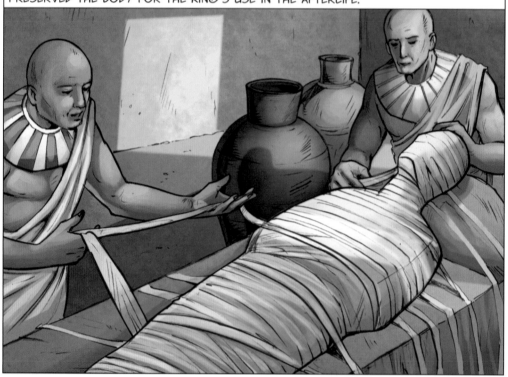

THE MUMMIFIED BODY WAS PLACED IN A STONE BOX WITHIN THE PYRAMID. AFTER THE PROPER PRAYERS WERE SAID, THE DOORS WERE CLOSED AND SEALED FOR **ETERNITY**.

AFTER THE WORK OF THE DAY WAS DONE, EGYPTIAN FAMILIES RELAXED AT HOME. IMHOTEP'S MOTHER AND SISTERS PLAYED A GAME CALLED SENET. IMHOTEP PRACTICED HIS WRITING, WHILE HIS YOUNGER BROTHERS PLAYED OUTSIDE.

BEING A SCRIBE IS THE FIRST STEP TO BECOMING AN ARCHITECT.

LOOK, FATHER! I HAVE WRITTEN THE KING'S NAME.

EACH DAY IS LIKE THE NILE, RISING AND FALLING.

YES, THE SUN COMES UP, THE SUN GOES DOWN.

THERE IS, AND WILL ALWAYS BE, BALANCE AND ORDER IN THE LAND.

DAY IN AND DAY OUT, THE PATTERN OF LIFE IN EGYPT CONTINUES.

EVEN WHEN I AM AT SCHOOL, MY LIFE WILL FOLLOW THE PATTERN, RISING AND FALLING, ORDER AND BALANCE.

Did You Know?

- Historians divide ancient Egyptian history into several eras:

  Old Kingdom and First Intermediate Period (c. 2686–1991 BC) The Step Pyramid of Djoser and the great pyramids at Giza were built during this period. Pepi II was the last strong ruler of the Old Kingdom.

  Middle Kingdom and the Second Intermediate Period (c. 2060–1552 BC) During the Second Intermediate Period, foreign invaders brought the chariot to Egypt.

  New Kingdom (c. 1552–1069 BC) Famous kings of this period included Tutankhamen and Ramses II.

  Later dynasties and the Ptolemaic period (1069–30 BC) Foreign conquerors adopted Egyptian culture and customs. Cleopatra, who was actually Greek, was the last ruler of this period.

- The main pyramid of Pepi II is called Pepi Is Established and Alive. Its height is 172 feet (52 m). The Great Pyramid of Khufu is 481 feet (147 m) high.

- Egyptian hieroglyphic writing was used for almost 3,500 years.

- Egyptian gold workers made fine wire by pulling strips of gold through smaller and smaller holes.

- Most Egyptian buildings were made of sun-dried bricks.

Glossary

amulet (AM-yeh-let) Something worn as a good-luck charm.

apprentice (uh-PREN-tis) A person who learns a trade by working for someone who is already trained.

chaos (KAY-ahs) Complete lack of order.

decline (dih-KLYN) Becoming less in amount.

drought (DROWT) A period of dryness that causes harm to crops.

economic (eh-kuh-NAH-mik) Having to do with the way in which a country or a business oversees its goods and services.

eternity (ih-TUR-nuh-tee) Forever.

flax (FLAKS) A fiber that comes from the stem of the flax plant and that can be spun into thread to make a kind of cloth called linen.

funerary complex (FYOO-neh-rer-ee KOM-pleks) Buildings in which an Egyptian king or queen was buried along with the items he or she would need in the afterlife.

rituals (RIH-choo-ulz) Special series of actions done for reasons of faith.

scribes (SKRYBZ) People whose job is to copy books by hand.

shrine (SHRYN) A special place at which prayers or memorials can be made.

silt (SILT) Fine bits of earth, smaller than sand grains, found at the bottom of lakes and streams.

status (STA-tus) Someone's position compared to others.

tomb (TOOM) A grave.

Index

A
Anubis, 17
architect(s), 4, 10, 13–14, 20

B
barley, 6
Black Land, 3
bread, 5–7, 9

D
Djoser, 12
drought, 3

F
flax, 8
food, 5, 6, 7
funerary complex, 3

I
Imhotep, 12

K
ka, 11
kohl, 4

L
linen, 8

M
mummification, 19

N
Neith, 9
Nile, 3, 4, 14

P
Pepi II, 3, 12, 14, 16, 17
priestess, 9, 15

R
ritual(s), 3, 19

S
Sakkara, 3, 4
scribe(s), 10, 16, 20
shrine, 5

T
tomb, 11–12

Web Sites

Due to the changing nature of Internet links, PowerKids Press has developed an online list of Web sites related to the subject of this book. This site is updated regularly. Please use this link to access the list:

www.powerkidslinks.com/civi/egypt/